Look and See 1

ACTIVITY BOOK

Gregg Schroeder

NATIONAL GEOGRAPHIC
LEARNING

Australia • Brazil • Mexico • Singapore • United Kingdom • United States

Look and See 1

ACTIVITY BOOK

1 TR: 0.1 Listen and point.

2 TR: 0.2 Sing and do.

3 Draw and say.

UNIT 1 Hello!

1 TR: 1.1 Listen. Circle ✔ or ✘.

1 (✔) ✘

2 ✔ ✘

3 ✔ ✘

4 ✔ ✘

5 ✔ ✘

6 ✔ ✘

2 Point and say.

1

2

3

NEW WORDS: *Hello! Goodbye. Say hello. Wave goodbye. Stand up. Sit down. Open your book. Close your book.*

1 TR: 1.2 Listen and circle.

1

2

3

1 TR: 1.3 Sing and point.

2 Look and circle.

VALUE **Make friends.**

1

2

1 Trace.

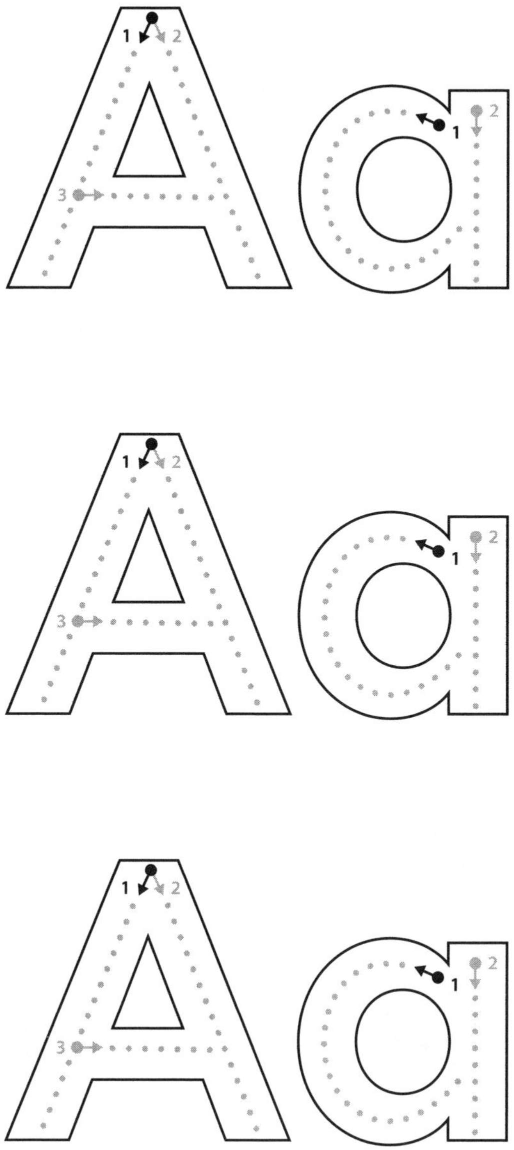

2 Draw yourself.

UNIT

2 School

1 TR: 2.1 Listen and circle.

1

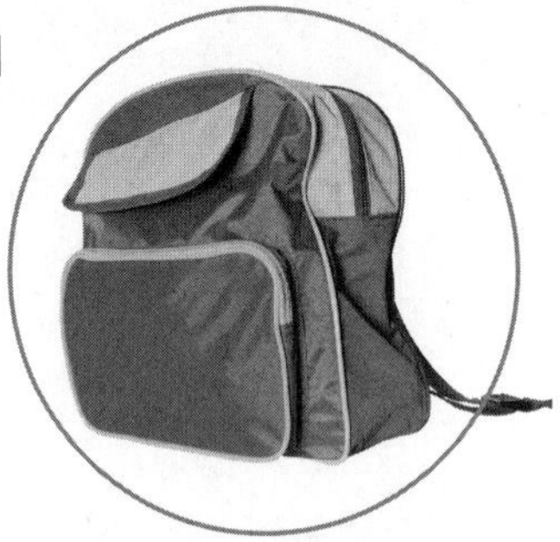

2

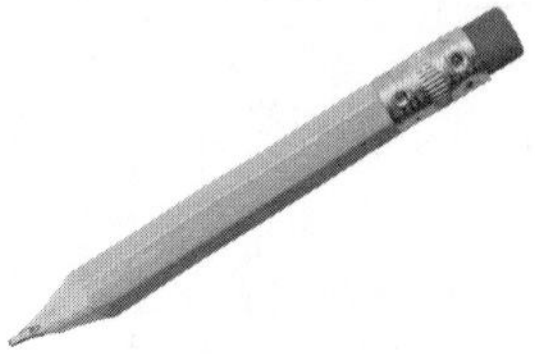

3

4

5

6

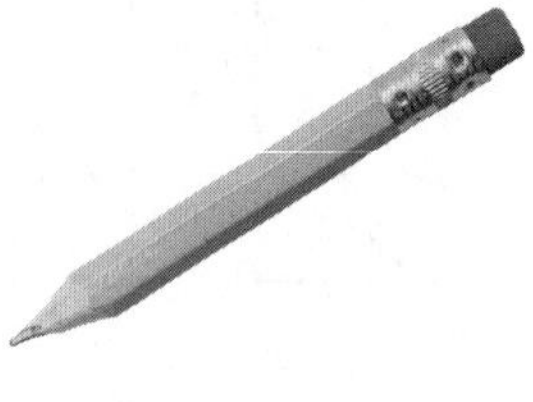

 NEW WORDS: *apron, bag, chair, crayon, pencil, school, table*

1 TR: 2.2 Listen. Circle ✔ or ✘.

1 ✔ ✘

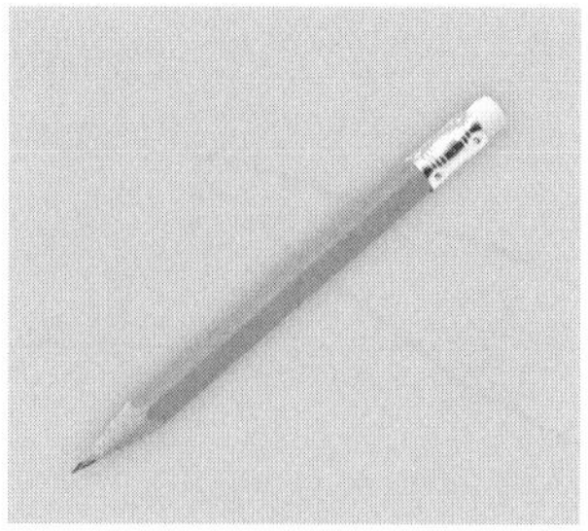

2 ✔ ✘

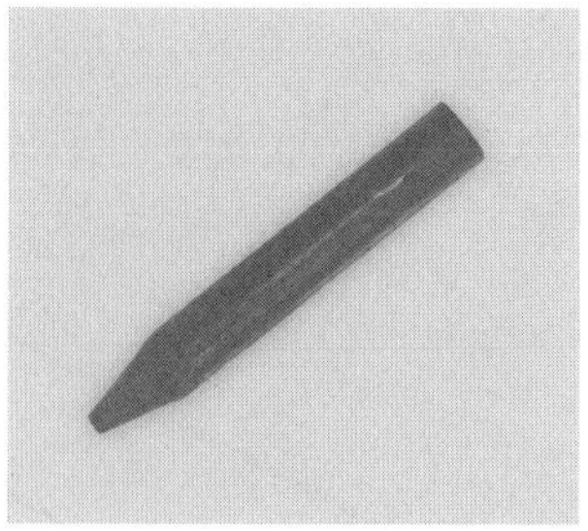

3 ✔ ✘

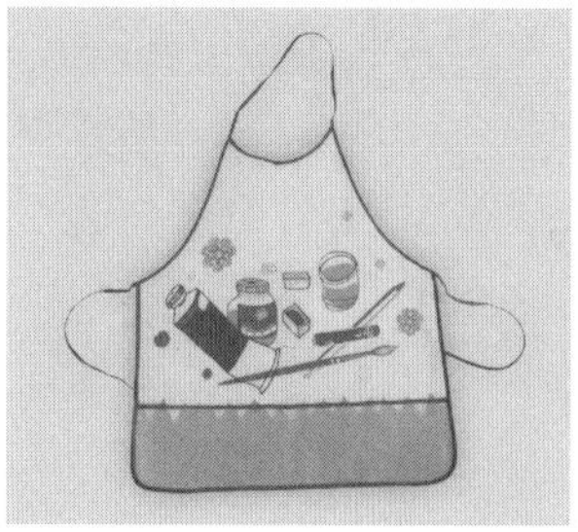

4 ✔ ✘

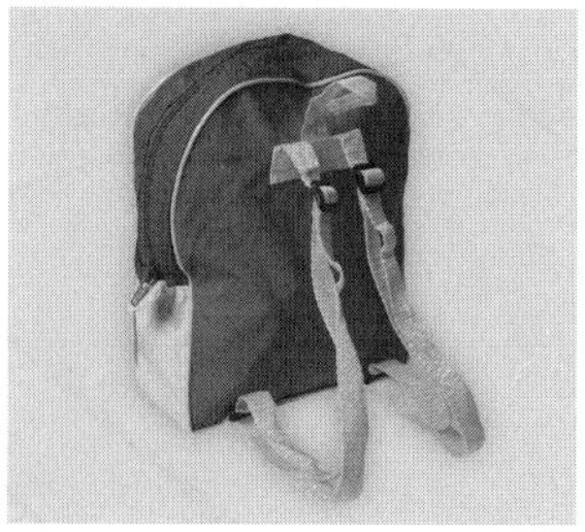

5 ✔ ✘

2 Color. Ask and answer.

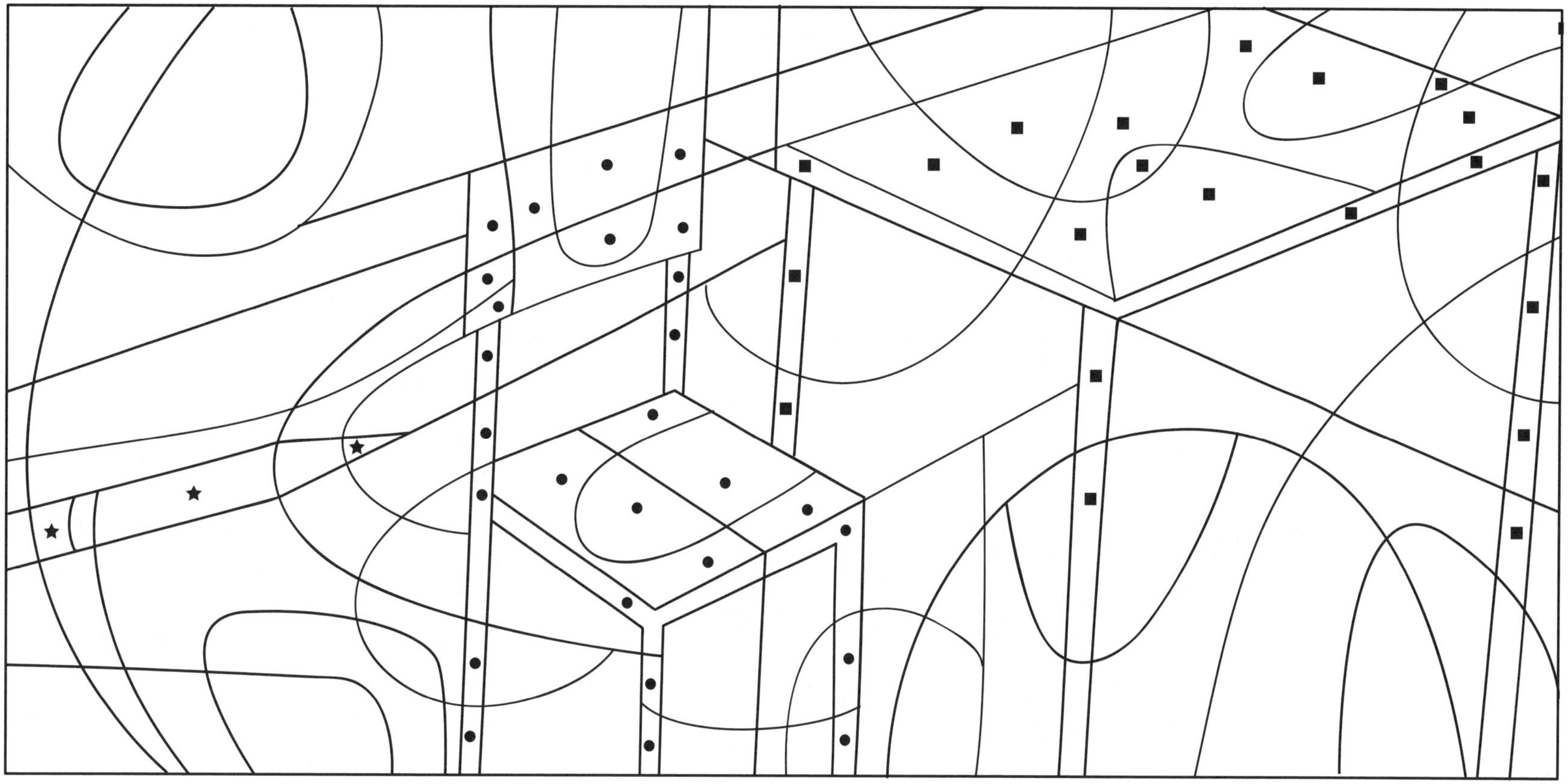

1 TR: 2.3 Color. Sing and point.

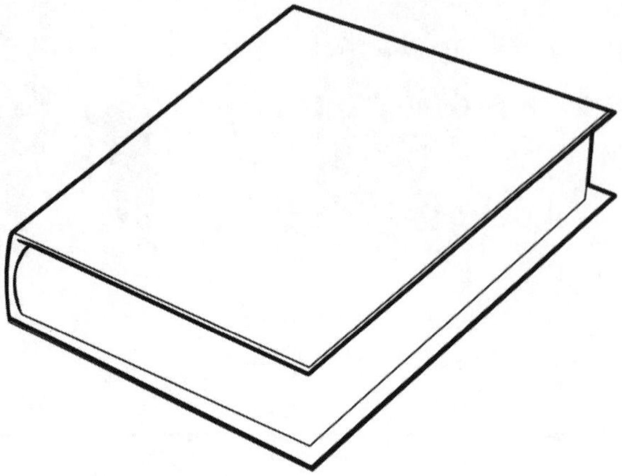

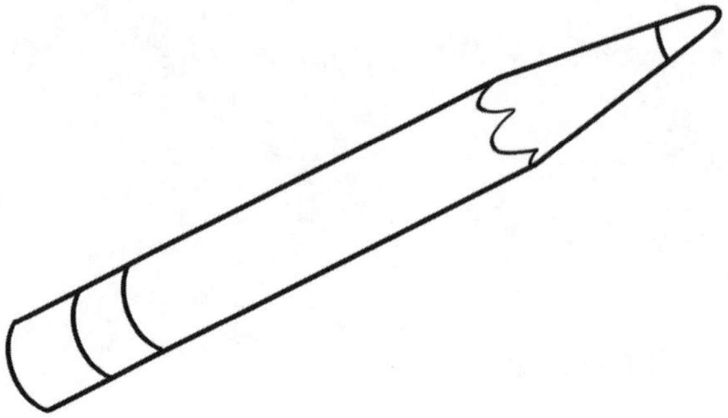

2 Look and circle.

VALUE **Take care of your things.**

1

2

1 Trace.

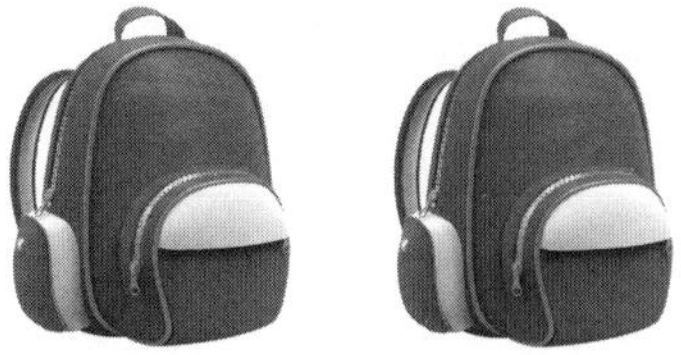

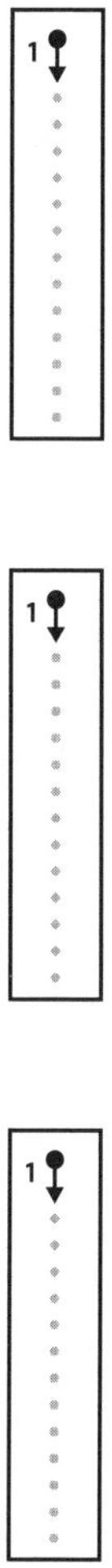

2 Draw your school.

UNIT

3 Colors

1 TR: 3.1 Listen and color.

1

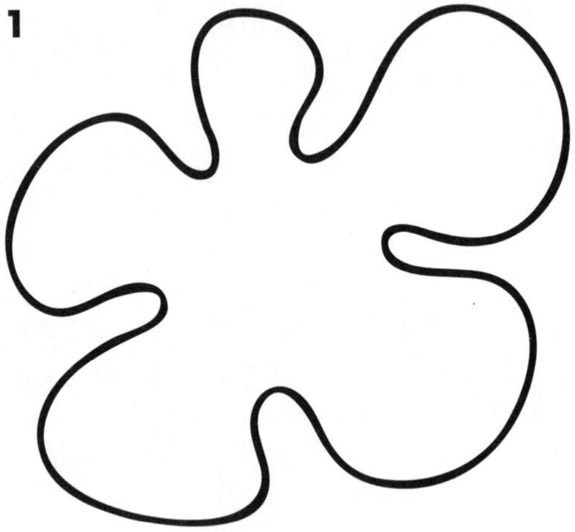

2

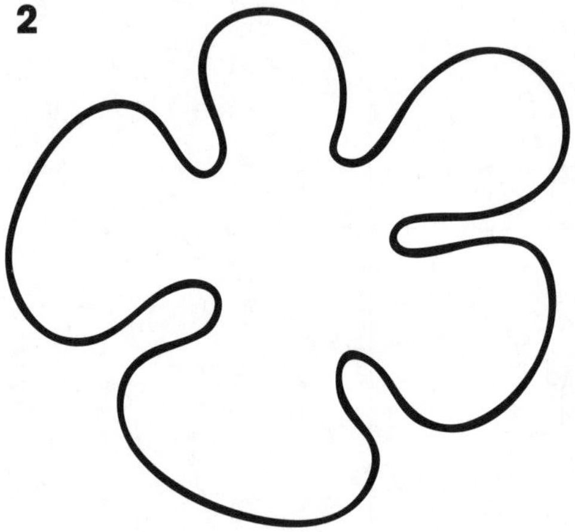

3

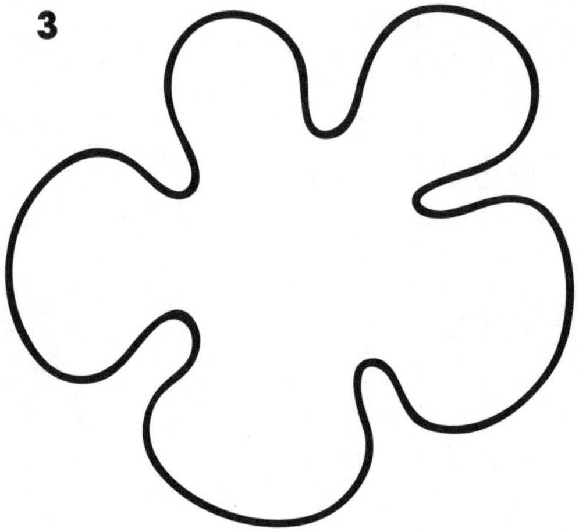

4

5

6

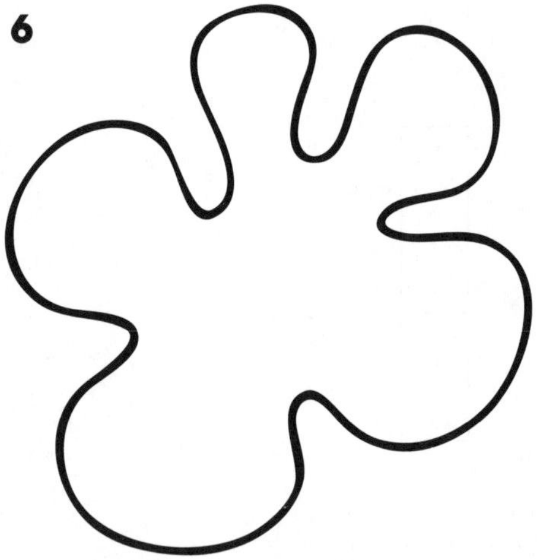

 NEW WORDS: *blue, green, orange, paint, purple, red, yellow*

1 TR: 3.2 Listen and color. Then ask and answer.

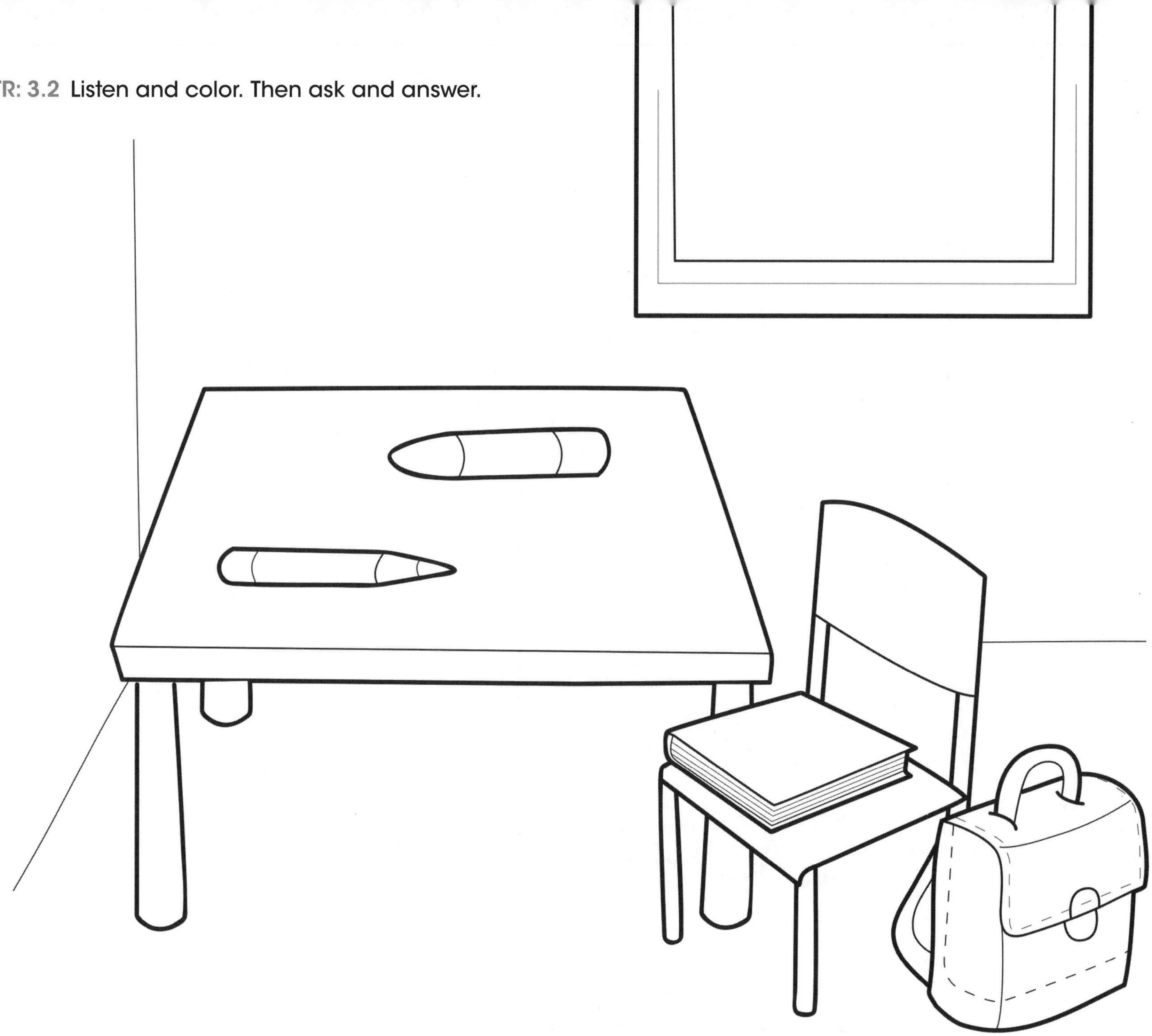

STRUCTURE: *What color is the book? It's red.*

1 TR: 3.3 Color. Sing and point.

2 Look and circle.

VALUE **Be creative.**

1

2

1 Trace.

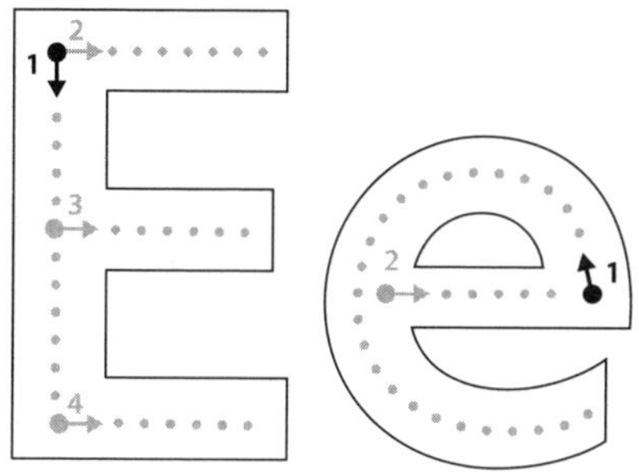

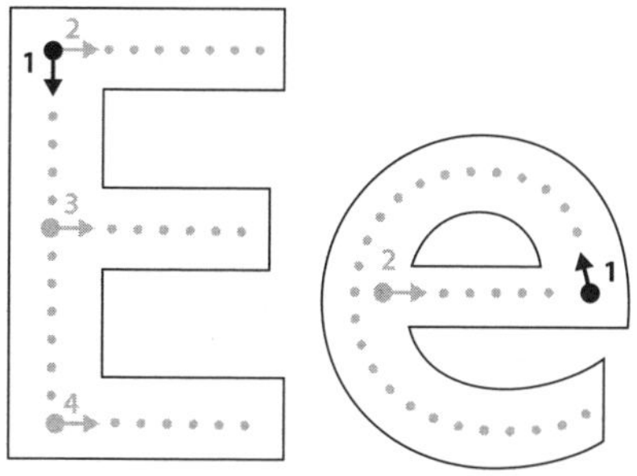

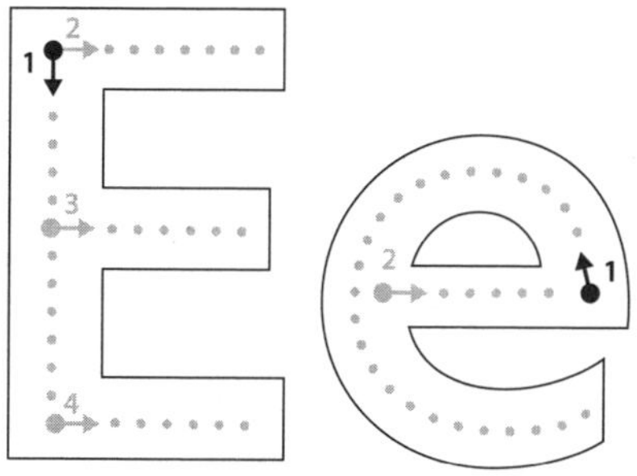

2 TR: 3.4 Listen and color.

1

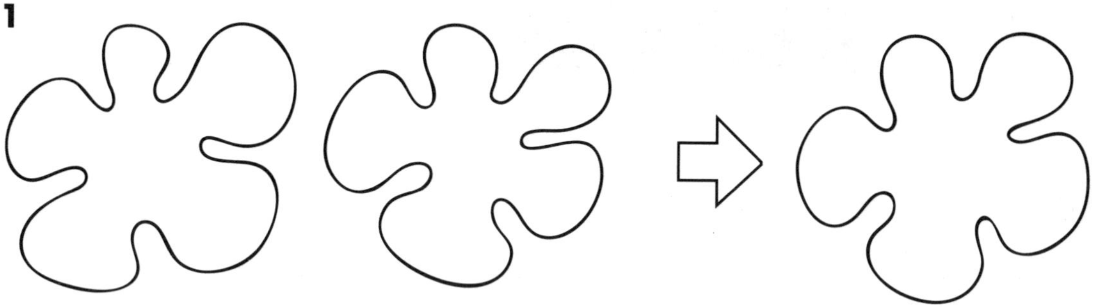

2

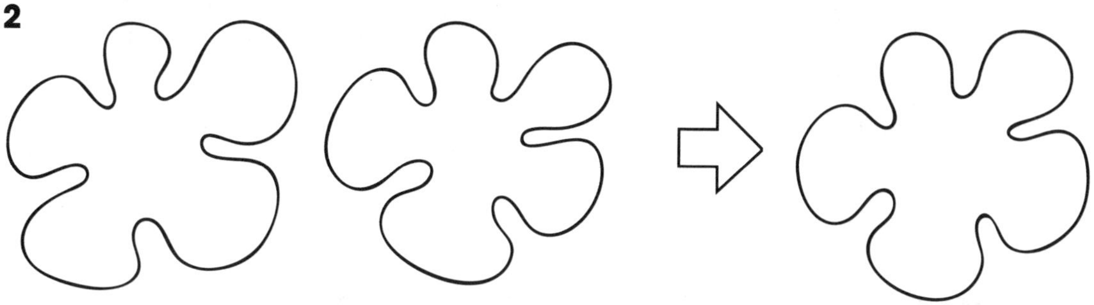

3

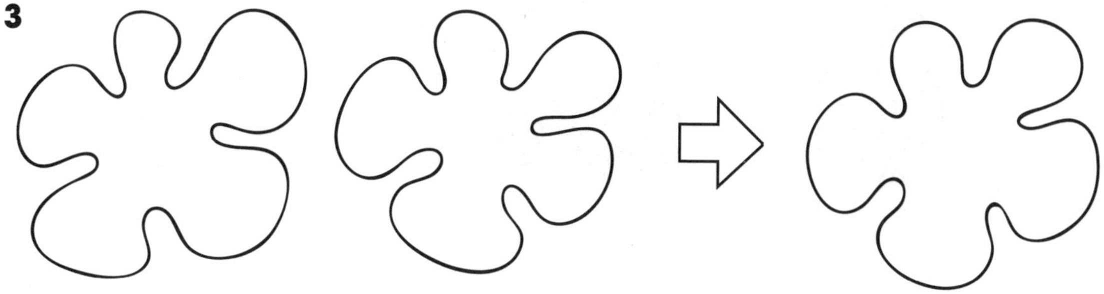

UNIT 4 Toys

1 TR: 4.1 Listen. Circle ✔ or ✘.

1 (✔) ✘

2 ✔ ✘

3 ✔ ✘

4 ✔ ✘

5 ✔ ✘

6 ✔ ✘

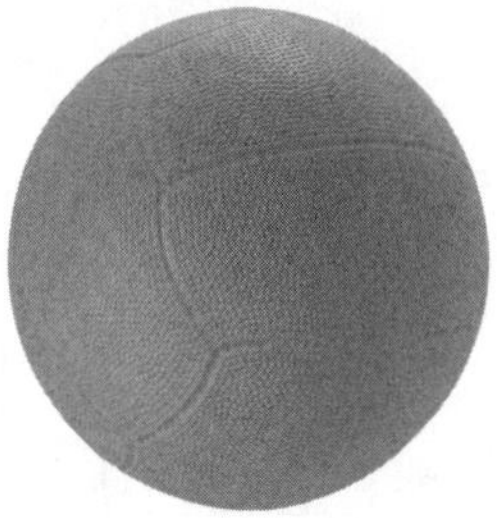

2 Color. Then point and say.

1

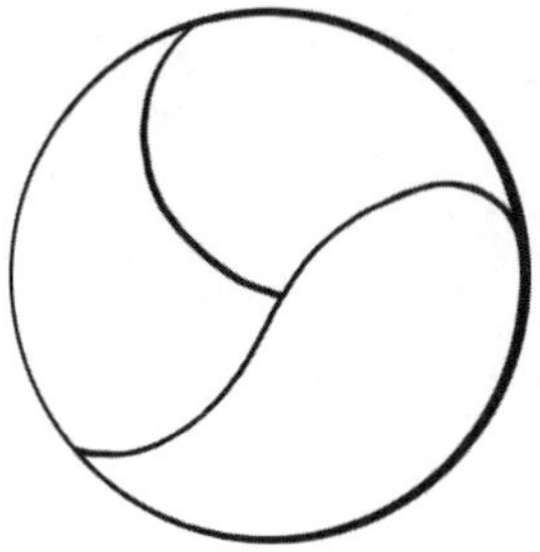

2

3

 NEW WORDS: *ball, bus, car, doll, puppet, teddy bear, train*

1 TR: 4.2 Listen and circle.

1

2

1 TR: 4.3 Listen, point, and count. Then color.

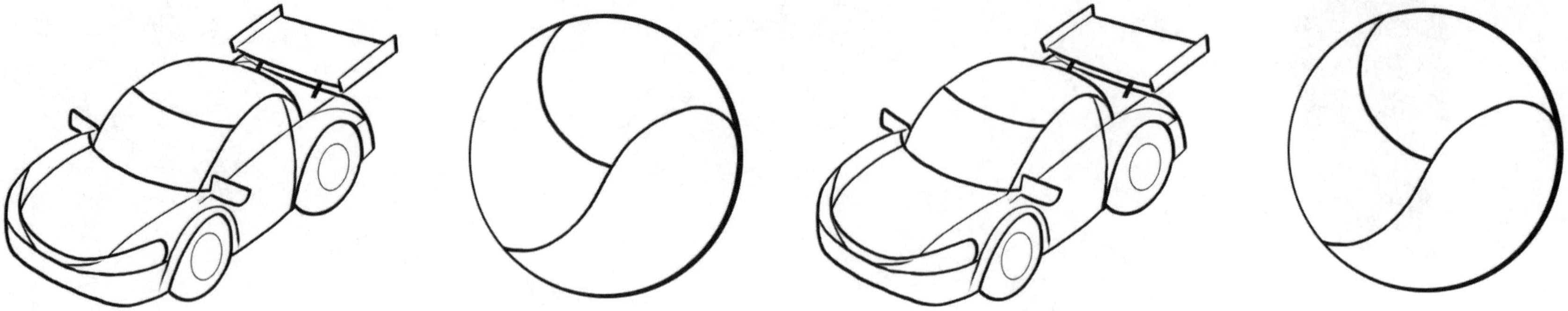

2 Look and circle.

VALUE **Share your toys.**

1

2

1 Trace.

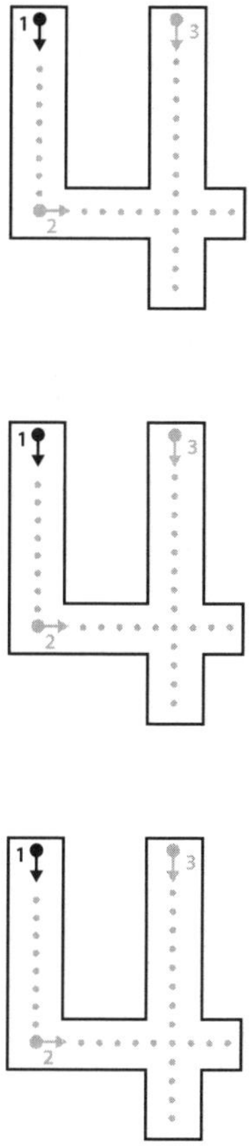

2 Draw your favorite toy.

UNIT

5 Let's Move!

1 TR: 5.1 Listen and point.

2 Trace and say. Then color.

NEW WORDS: *arms, body, feet, hands, head, legs, tummy*

1 Play and say. Then do.

Heads: Move 1

Tails: Move 2

1 TR: 5.2 Listen and color. Then sing.

2 Look and circle.

VALUE **Be active.**

1

2

1 Trace.

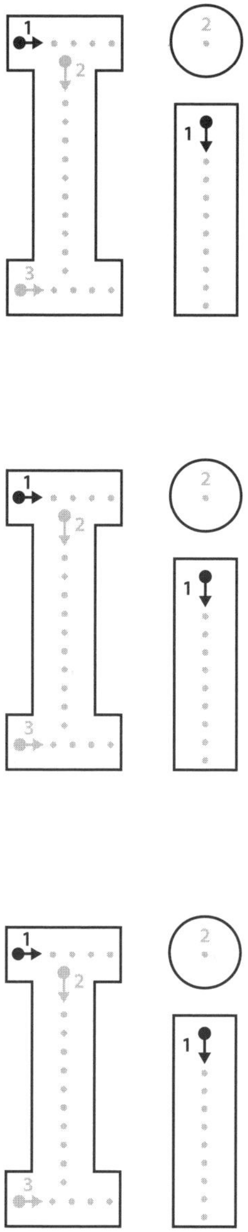

2 TR: 5.3 Listen and point.

1

2

3

UNIT 6 Food

1 TR: 6.1 Listen and circle.

1
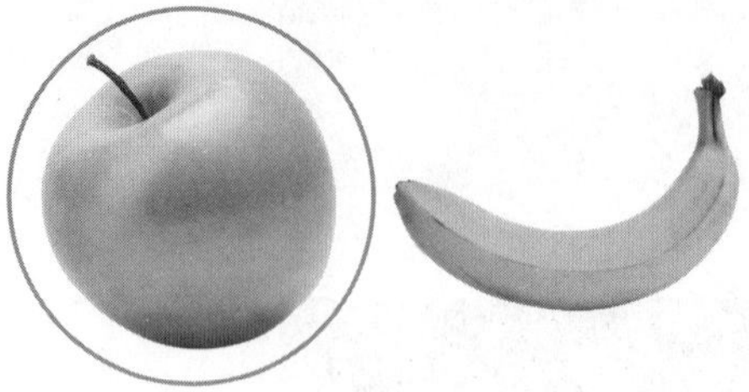

2

3

4

5

6

2 Color. Then point and say.

 NEW WORDS: *apple, banana, carrot, cracker, milk, orange, water*

1 TR: 6.2 Listen and circle.

1

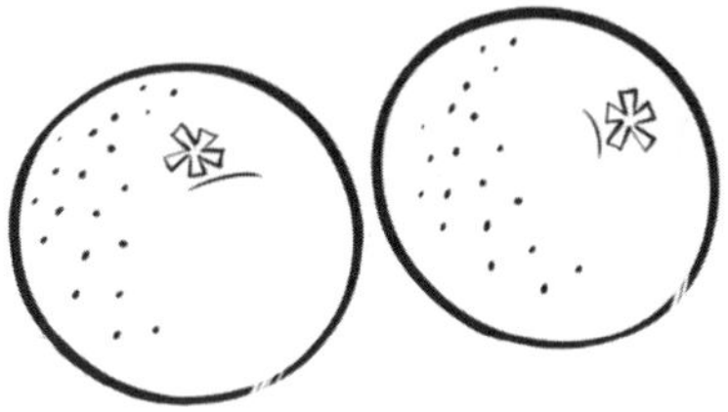

2

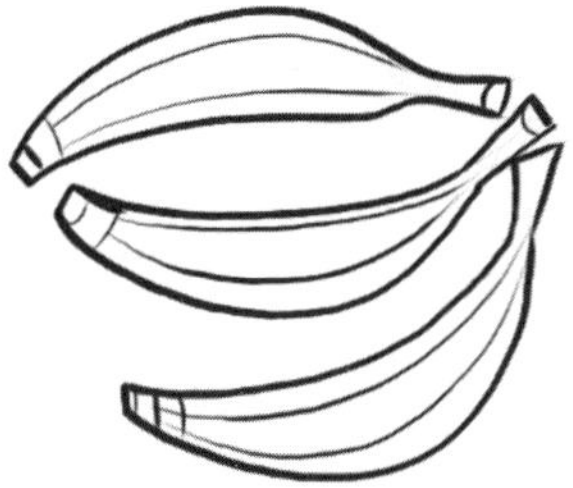

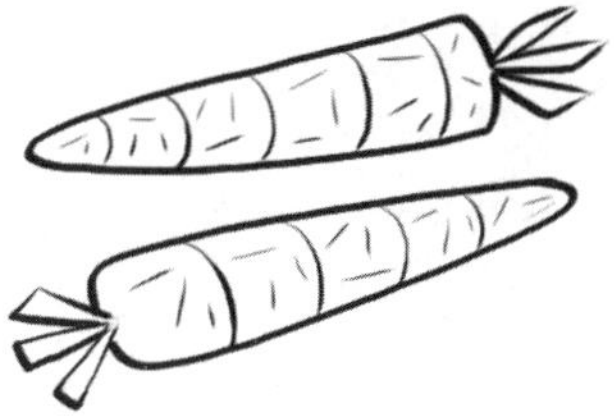

1 TR: 6.3 Listen and color. Then sing and point.

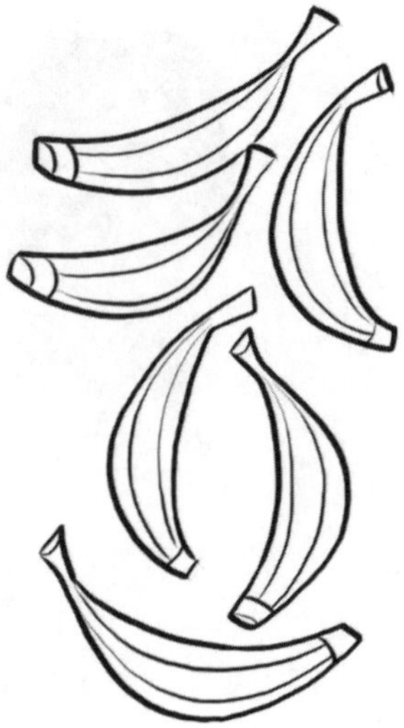

2 Look and circle.

VALUE **Choose healthy food.**

1

2

1 Trace.

2 Draw your favorite tree.

UNIT 7 My Family

1 TR: 7.1 Listen and match.

1

2

3

A

B

C

2 Point and say.

 NEW WORDS: *brother, dad, grandma, grandpa, mom, photo, sister*

1 Draw your family and say. Then color.

1 TR: 7.2 Listen and match. Then sing.

2 Look and circle.

VALUE **Be good to your family.**

1

2

3

1 Trace.

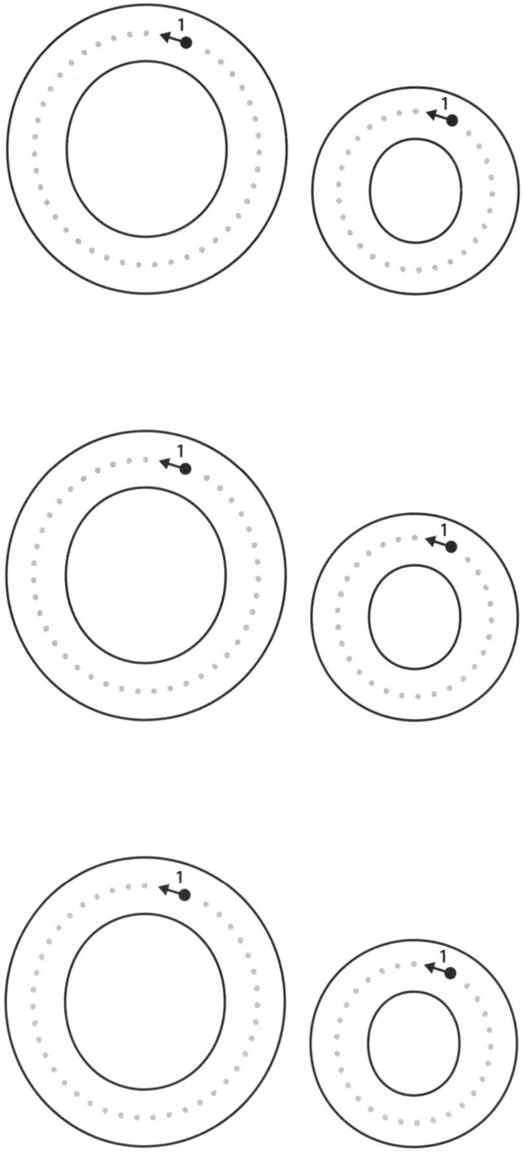

2 TR: 7.3 Listen and match.

1 **2**

UNIT
8 On the Farm

1 TR: 8.1 Listen. Circle ✔ or ✘.

1 ✔ ✘

2 ✔ ✘

3 ✔ ✘

4 ✔ ✘

5 ✔ ✘

6 ✔ ✘

7 ✔ ✘

2 Match and say.

1

2

3

4

A

B

C

D

NEW WORDS: *cat, chicken, cow, dog, goat, horse, sheep*

1 TR: 8.2 Listen. Circle ✔ or ✘.

1 ✔ ✘

2 ✔ ✘

3 ✔ ✘

4 ✔ ✘

5 ✔ ✘

2 Ask and answer.

1

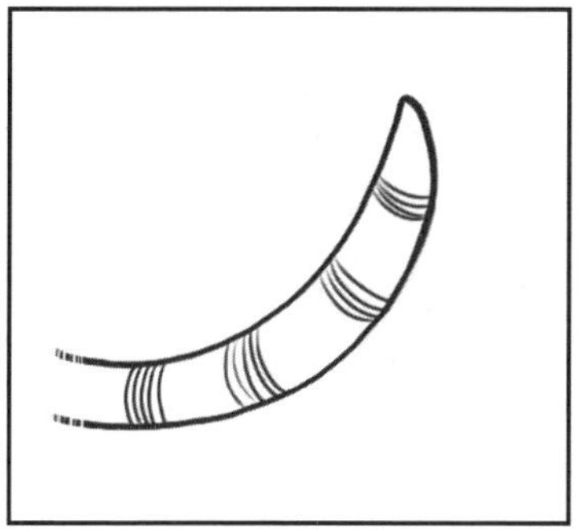

2

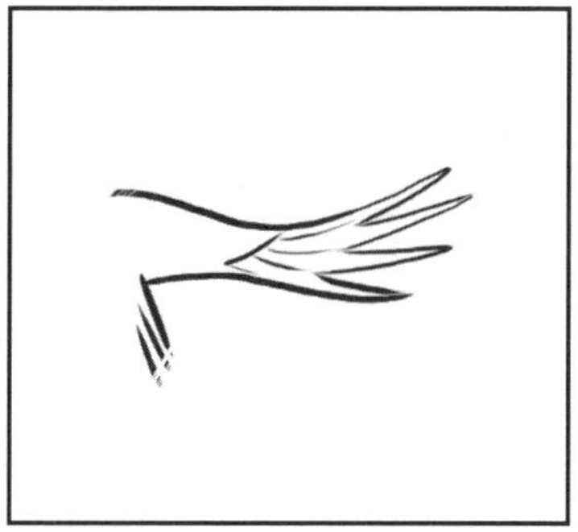

3

4

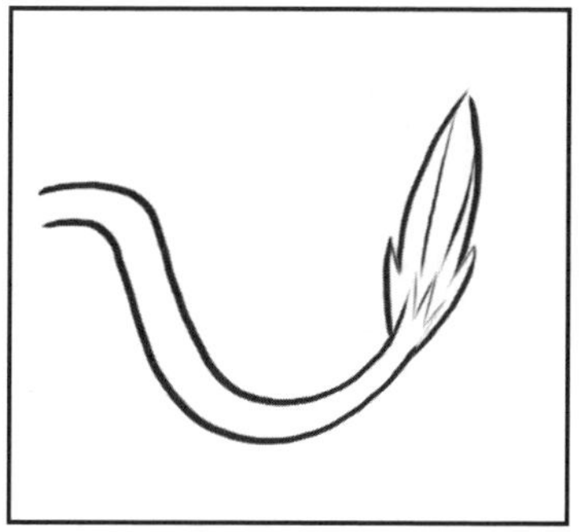

STRUCTURE: *Is it a cow? No, it isn't. Is it a horse? Yes, it is.*

1 TR: 8.3 Sing and point.

2 Look and circle.

VALUE **Take care of animals.**

1

2

3

1 Trace.

2 Match and say.

1

A

2

B

3

C

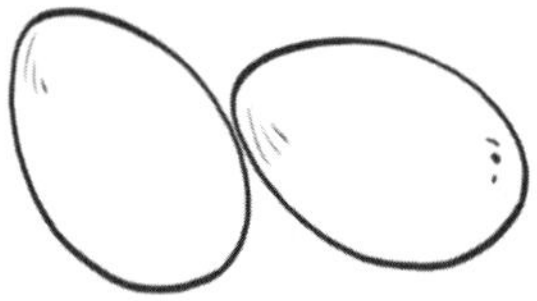

UNIT

9 My Clothes

1 TR: 9.1 Listen and match.

1 **2** **3** **4** **5** **6**

2 TR: 9.2 Listen and color.

1 
2 
3 
4 
5 
6 

 NEW WORDS: *hat, jacket, shoes, shorts, socks, T-shirt; black, brown, white*

1 TR: 9.3 Listen and color. Then match and say.

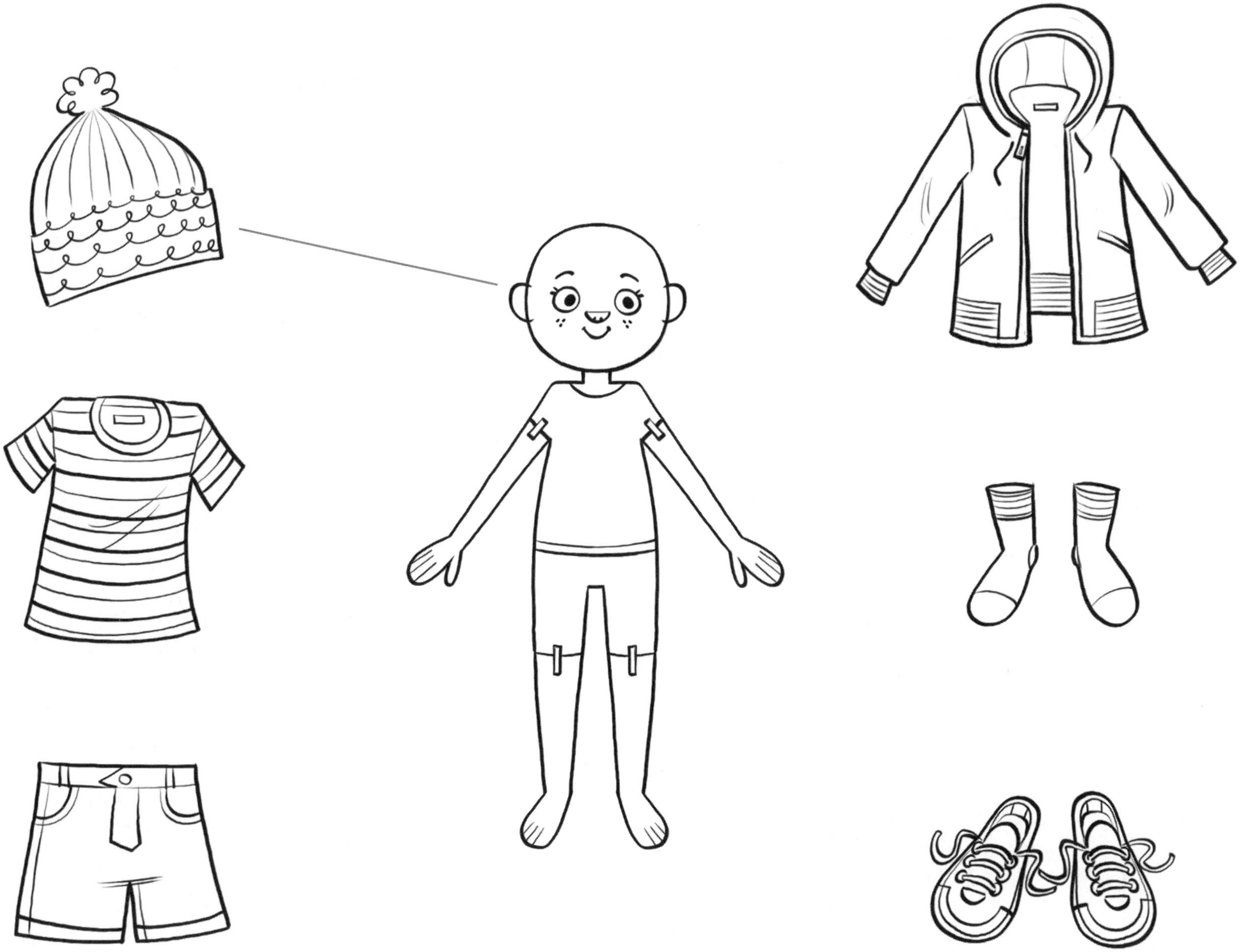

STRUCTURE: *My T-shirt is orange. My shorts are red.*

1 TR: 9.4 Listen and color. Then sing.

2 Look and circle.

VALUE **Dress yourself.**

1

2

3

1 Trace.

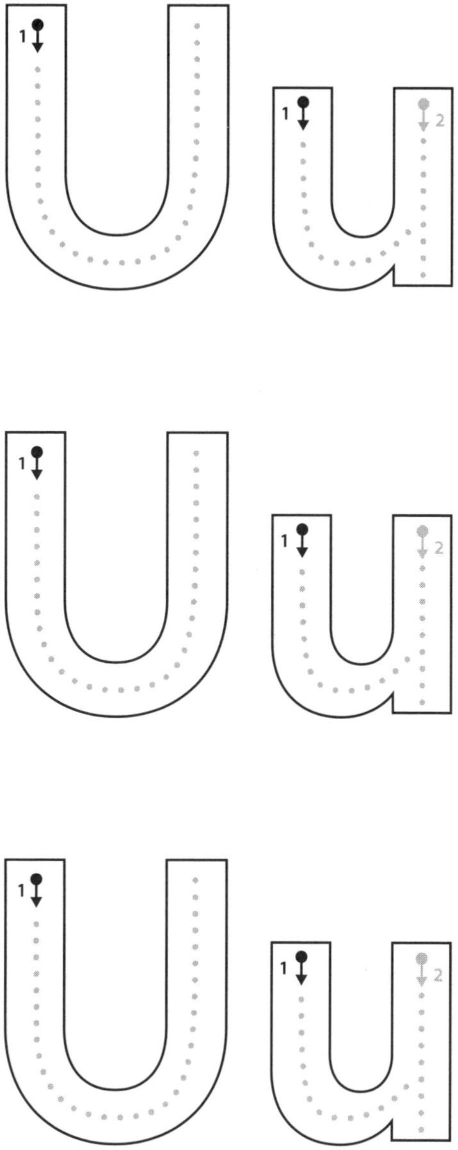

2 Trace, match, and say.

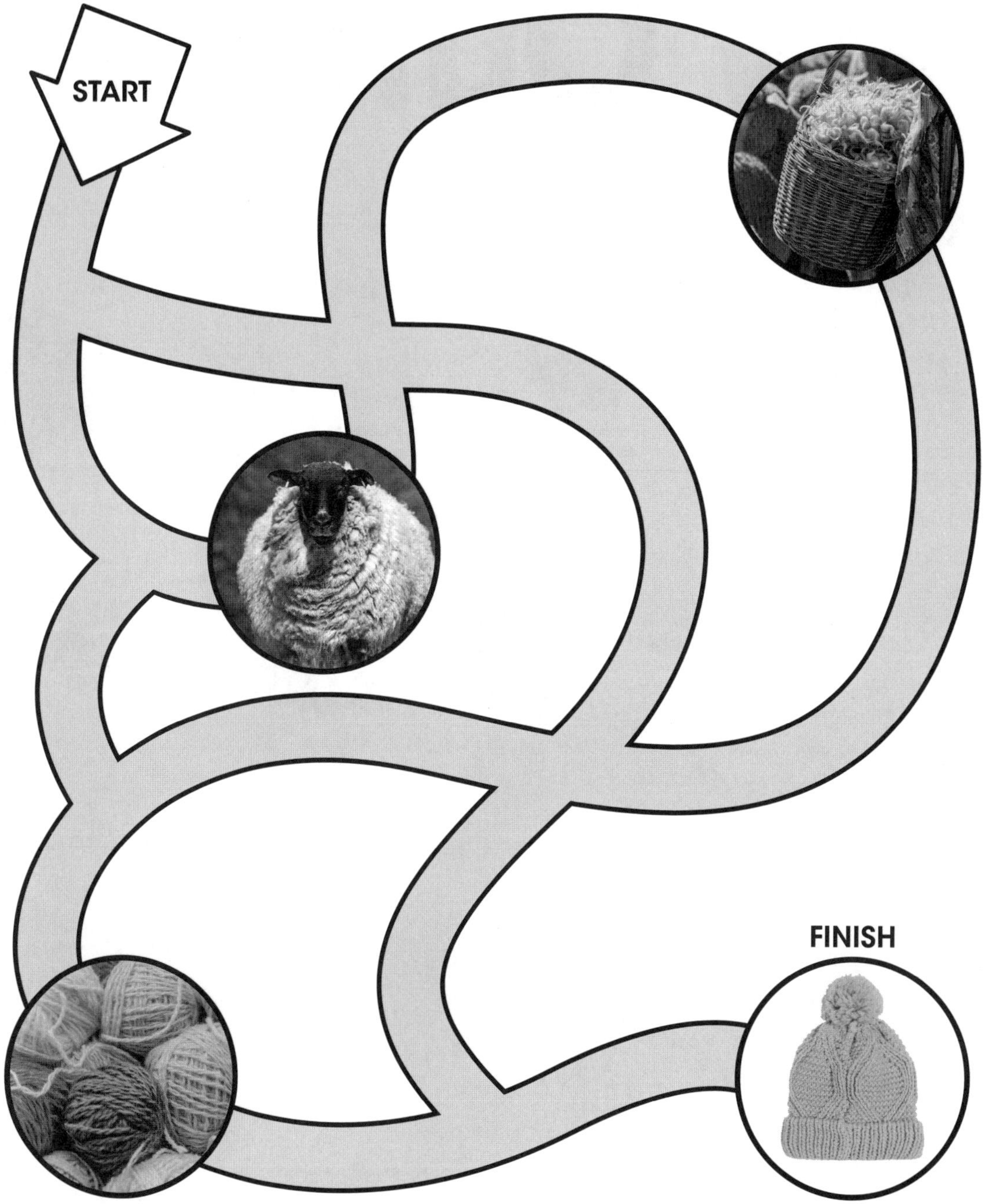

UNIT

10 Outside

1 TR: 10.1 Listen and circle.

1

2

3

4

5

6

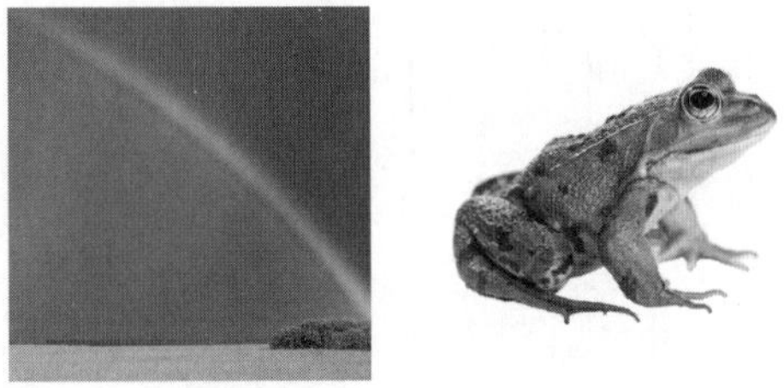

2 Point and say.

NEW WORDS: *bird, fish, flower, frog, leaf, rainbow, tree*

1 TR: 10.2 Listen and circle. Then find.

(1) 2 3

1 2 3

1 2 3

4 5 6

4 5 6

6 7 8

6 7 8

1 TR: 10.3 Listen and circle. Then sing.

1 2 3

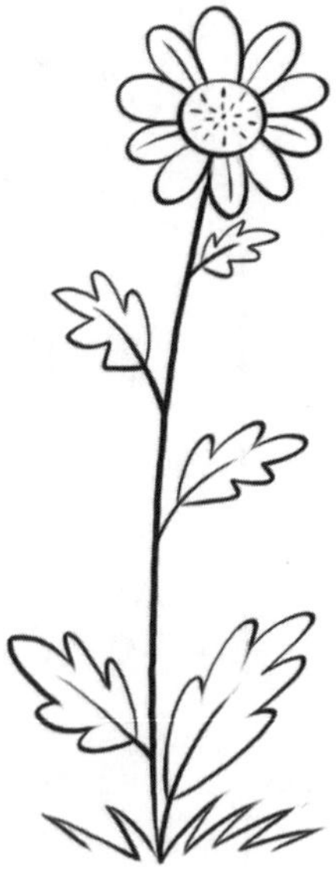

3 4 5

2 Look and circle.

VALUE **Explore outside.**

1

2

3

1 Trace.

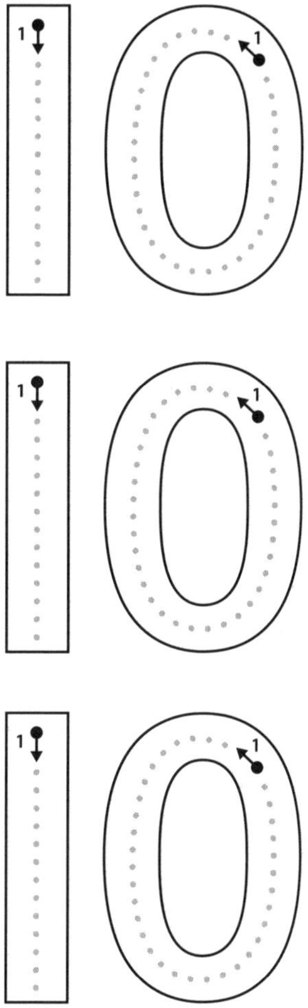

2 TR: 10.4 Listen and color.

1

2

3

CREDITS

PHOTOS: 6 (tl) Kativ/E+/Getty Images; (tm) David Hanson/Aurora Photos; (tr) paultarasenko/Shutterstock.com; (bl) AustinandAugust/Shutterstock.com; (bm) praetorianphoto/iStock/Getty Images; (br) Tetra Images, LLC/Alamy Stock Photo; **10** (tl) ZouZou/Shutterstock.com; (tml) iprachenko/Shutterstock.com; (tmr) Mega Pixel/Shutterstock.com; (tr) John Kasawa/Shutterstock.com; (ml) Lucie Lang/Shutterstock.com; (mml) Juris Kraulis/Alamy Stock Photo; (mmr) iprachenko/Shutterstock.com; (mr) John Kasawa/Shutterstock.com; (bl) Juris Kraulis/Alamy Stock Photo; (bml) ZouZou/Shutterstock.com; (bmr) Mega Pixel/Shutterstock.com; (br) Lucie Lang/Shutterstock.com; **11** (ml) chalrumpon onnongwa/Shutterstock.com; (mml) daizuoxin/Shutterstock.com; (m) Natalya Erofeeva/Shutterstock.com; (mr) Hurst Photo/Shutterstock.com; (r) Monkey Business Images/Shutterstock.com; **13** Sergiy Tryapitsyn/Alamy Stock Photo; **18** (tl) Sintez/iStock/Getty Images; (tm) kyoshino/iStock/Getty Images; (tr) Dorling Kindersley ltd/Alamy Stock Photo; (bl) CykOtie/Shutterstock.com; (bm) Andrea Donetti/EyeEm/Getty Images; (br) taweesak thiprod/Shutterstock.com; **21** Twin Design/Shutterstock.com; **23** (tl) VOJTa Herout/Shutterstock.com; (tr) VOJTa Herout/Shutterstock.com; (mtl) Westend61 GmbH/Alamy Stock Photo; (mtm) Dave King/Dorling Kindersley/Getty Images; (mtr) Apichet Chakreeyarut/Alamy Stock Photo; (bml) ViewStock/Getty Images; (bmm) Werli Francois/Alamy Stock Photo; (bmr) Karen Anderson/Moment Open/Getty Images; (bl) sarahwolfephotography/Moment/Getty Images; (br) Maisie Paterson/Tetra images/Getty Images; **25** (t) Erdark/Vetta/Getty Images; (m) AP Archive; (b) Perinjo/Creatas Video/Getty Images; **26** (tl) CWIS/Shutterstock.com; (tml) Sergey Ivanychev/EyeEm/Getty Images; (tmr) Tarasyuk Igor/Shutterstock.com; (tr) Danny Smythe/Shutterstock.com; (ml) Cheers Group/Shutterstock.com; (mml) Valentina Razumova/Shutterstock.com; (mmr) Jiri Hera/Shutterstock.com; (mr) Sergey Ivanychev/EyeEm/Getty Images; (bl) Danny Smythe/Shutterstock.com; (bml) Valentina Razumova/Shutterstock.com; (bmr) Cheers Group/Shutterstock.com; (br) CWIS/Shutterstock.com; **29** (l) Cheers Group/Shutterstock.com; (r) Sergey Ivanychev/EyeEm/Getty Images; **30** (all) subodhsathe/iStock/Getty Images; **33** (t) blickwinkel/Alamy Stock Photo; (b) Blaine Harrington III/Alamy Stock Photo; **34** (l) Xuanyu Han/Moment/Getty Images; (ml) Evgeniy Zhukov/Shutterstock.com; (mml) pirita/Shutterstock.com; (m) IonelV/Shutterstock.com; (mmr) yuris/Shutterstock.com; (mr) MiaQu/Shutterstock.com; (r) Matteo Fagiolino/Moment/Getty Images; **35** (tl) pirita/Shutterstock.com; (tm) yuris/Shutterstock.com; (tr) MiaQu/Shutterstock.com; (bl) Xuanyu Han/Moment/Getty Images; (br) Evgeniy Zhukov/Shutterstock.com; **37** (l) Kuznetsov Alexey/Shutterstock.com; (r) Valentina_S/Shutterstock.com; **38** (l) Nanisimova/Shutterstock.com; (ml) PhotoAlto/Laurence Mouton/PhotoAlto Agency RF Collections/Getty Images; (mml) New Africa/Shutterstock.com; (mmr) SakisPagonas/Shutterstock.com; (mr) Iuliia Syrotina/Shutterstock.com; (r) TerraceStudio/Shutterstock.com; **41** (t) Norbert Scanella/Robert Harding; (m) andreac77/Shutterstock.com; (bl) elina.nova/Shutterstock.com; (br) gogoiso/Shutterstock.com; **42** (tl) Eric Isselee/Shutterstock.com; (tml) KasperczakBohdan/Shutterstock.com; (tmml) Ian 2010/Shutterstock.com; (tmmr) rsooll/Shutterstock.com; (tmr) Pavaphon Supanantananont/Shutterstock.com; (tr) Eric Isselee/Shutterstock.com; (bl) Pavaphon Supanantananont/Shutterstock.com; (bml) rsooll/Shutterstock.com; (bmml) KasperczakBohdan/Shutterstock.com; (bmmr) Ian 2010/Shutterstock.com; (bmr) Okhotnikova Ekaterina/Shutterstock.com; (br) Eric Isselee/Shutterstock.com; **45** (l) Fotofermer/Shutterstock.com; (r) Barbol/Shutterstock.com; **Back Cover** Joel Sartore/National Geographic Image Collection.

ILLUSTRATIONS: 4 Fabiana Faiallo; **6, 7, 8, 12, 14, 15, 16, 17, 18, 19, 20, 22, 24, 26, 27, 28, 30, 32, 34, 35, 36, 37, 38, 39, 40, 42, 43, 44, 45** Giovanni Giorgi Pierfranceschi.